KU-111-446

Teh Itteh Bitteh Book of Kittehs

TEH ITTE
BOOK OF

H BITTEH KITTEHS

A LOLcat Guide to Kittens

PROFESSOR HAPPYCAT and icanhascheezburger.com

summersdale

TEH ITTEH BITTEH BOOK OF KITTEHS

This edition published in 2011 by Summersdale Publishers Ltd.

First published in the USA in 2010 by Gotham Books Ltd, a member of Penguin Group (USA) Inc.

Copyright © Pet Holdings, Inc. 2010

All rights reserved.

No part of this book may be reproduced by any means, nor transmitted, nor translated into a machine language, without the written permission of both the copyright owner and the publishers.

Condition of Sale
This book is sold subject to the condition that it shall not, by way of trade or otherwise, be lent, re-sold, hired out or otherwise circulated in any form of binding or cover other than that in which it is published and without a similar condition including this condition being imposed on the subsequent publisher.

Summersdale Publishers Ltd
46 West Street
Chichester
West Sussex
PO19 1RP
UK

www.summersdale.com

Original design by Ben Gibson

Printed and bound in China

ISBN: 978-1-84953-182-5

While the authors have made every effort to provide accurate Internet addresses at the time of publication, neither the publisher nor the authors assume any responsibility for the errors, or for changes that occur after publication. Further, the publisher does not have any control over and does not assume responsibility for author or third-party websites or their content.

Substantial discounts on bulk quantities of Summersdale books are available to corporations, professional associations and other organisations. For details contact Summersdale Publishers by telephone: +44 (0) 1243 771107, fax: +44 (0) 1243 786300 or email: nicky@summersdale.com.

We dedicashuns dis buk to
all momcats ebberywhere.

CONTENTS

Momcat knows best

Uh-oh bad kitteh

Rules kittehs live bai

Itteh bitteh kitteh committeh hall of fame

crazy cat lady
teh early years

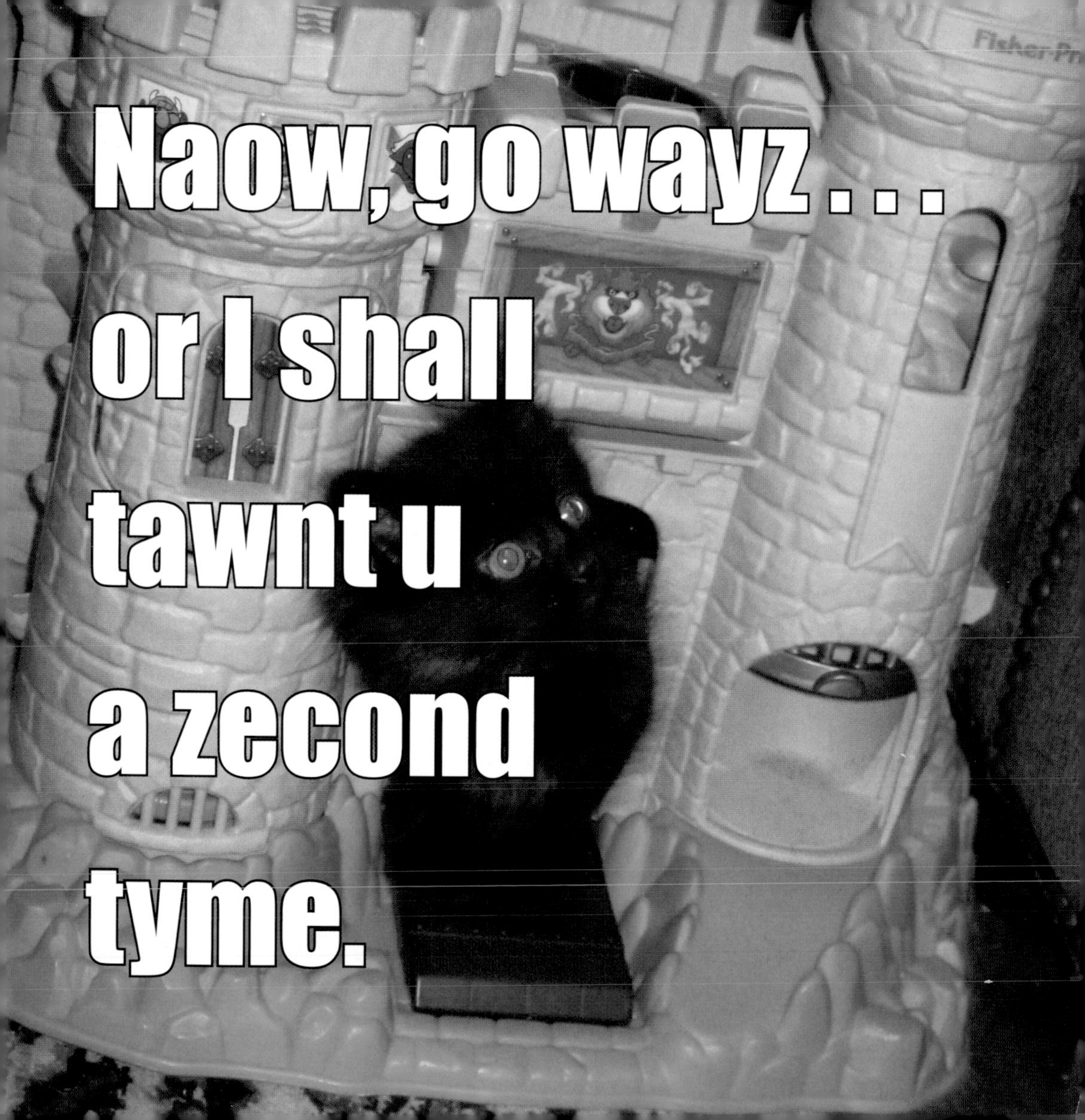
Naow, go wayz . . .
or I shall
tawnt u
a zecond
tyme.
Fisher-Pr

Halp . . . Iz ded . . . needz
bellywubs 2 resurect

quit hoverin, I can't write wif u watchin me

My furs gradeskool yrbook foto

Eye Exam: how many kitties do you see?

BEATING GAS PRICES
UR DOING IT WRONG

Ders monsterz under mai bed
kin I seep wif U?

Cat Starter Kit . . .
. . . Contents: 1

...tion   : CAT STARTER KIT
...ogue Number   : 870/6210(D)
... Number   : 273270
...items per outer : 1   set
... Origin   : China
...ght   : 4.5   kgs
...   : 3.5   kgs
...e   : 56x37x23 cm

KYOOTNESS: RESISTANCE IS FUTILE

shakespearean costume . . . on a budget

Dr. Tinycat's girlfrend Teeny

First
Kiss

My Grandma . . .
what a long nose you have.

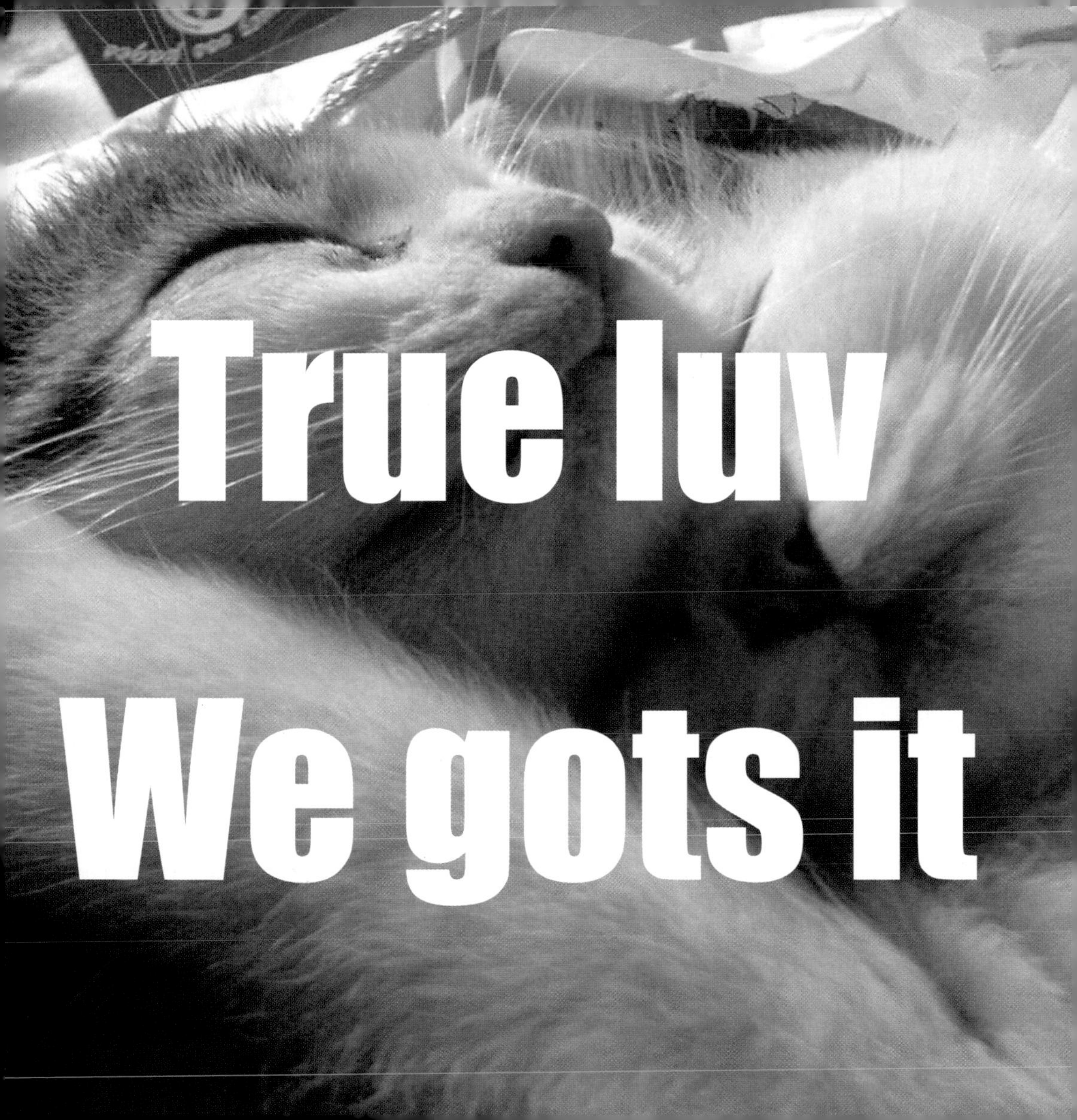
True luv
We gots it

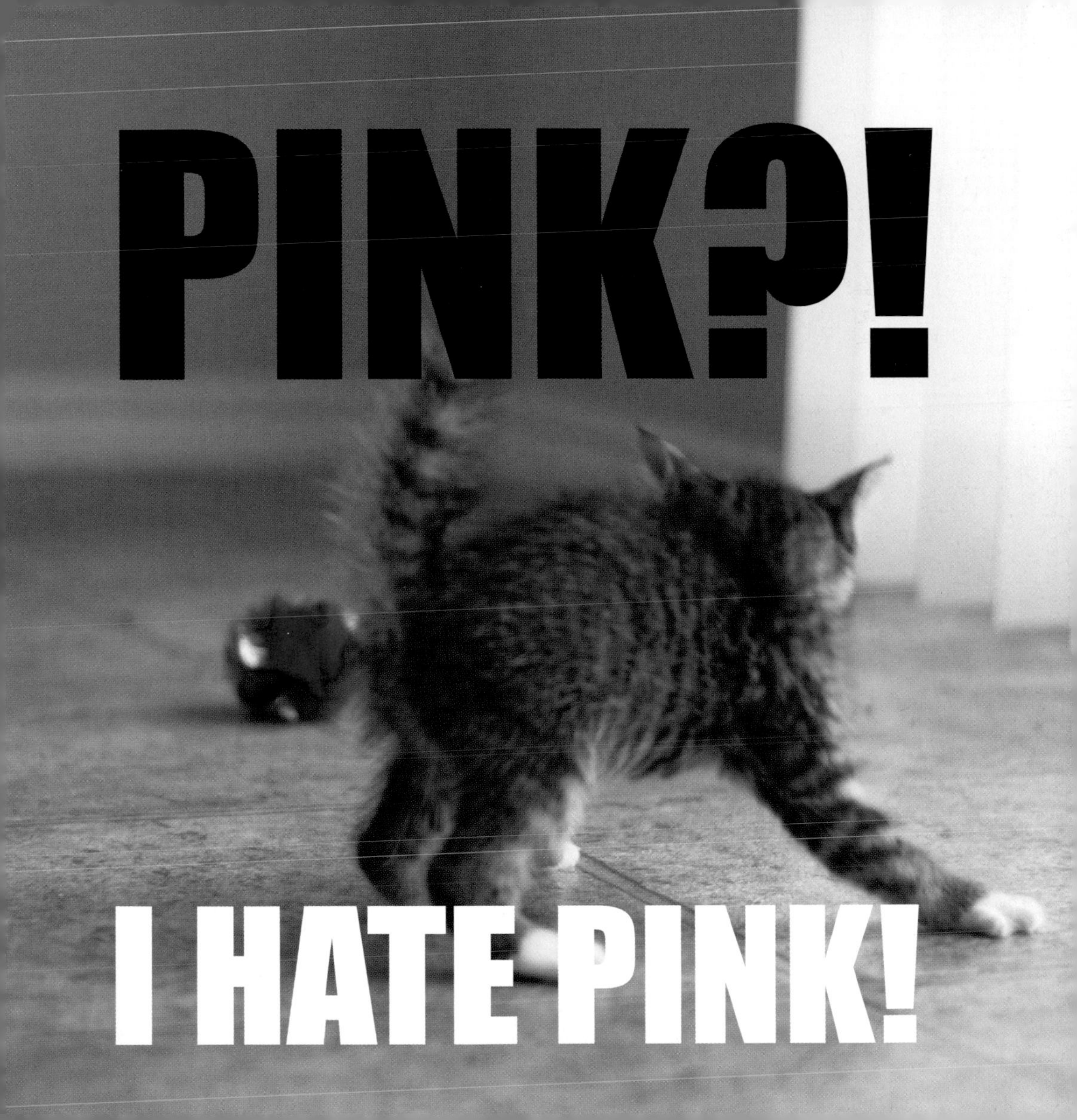
PINK?!
I HATE PINK!

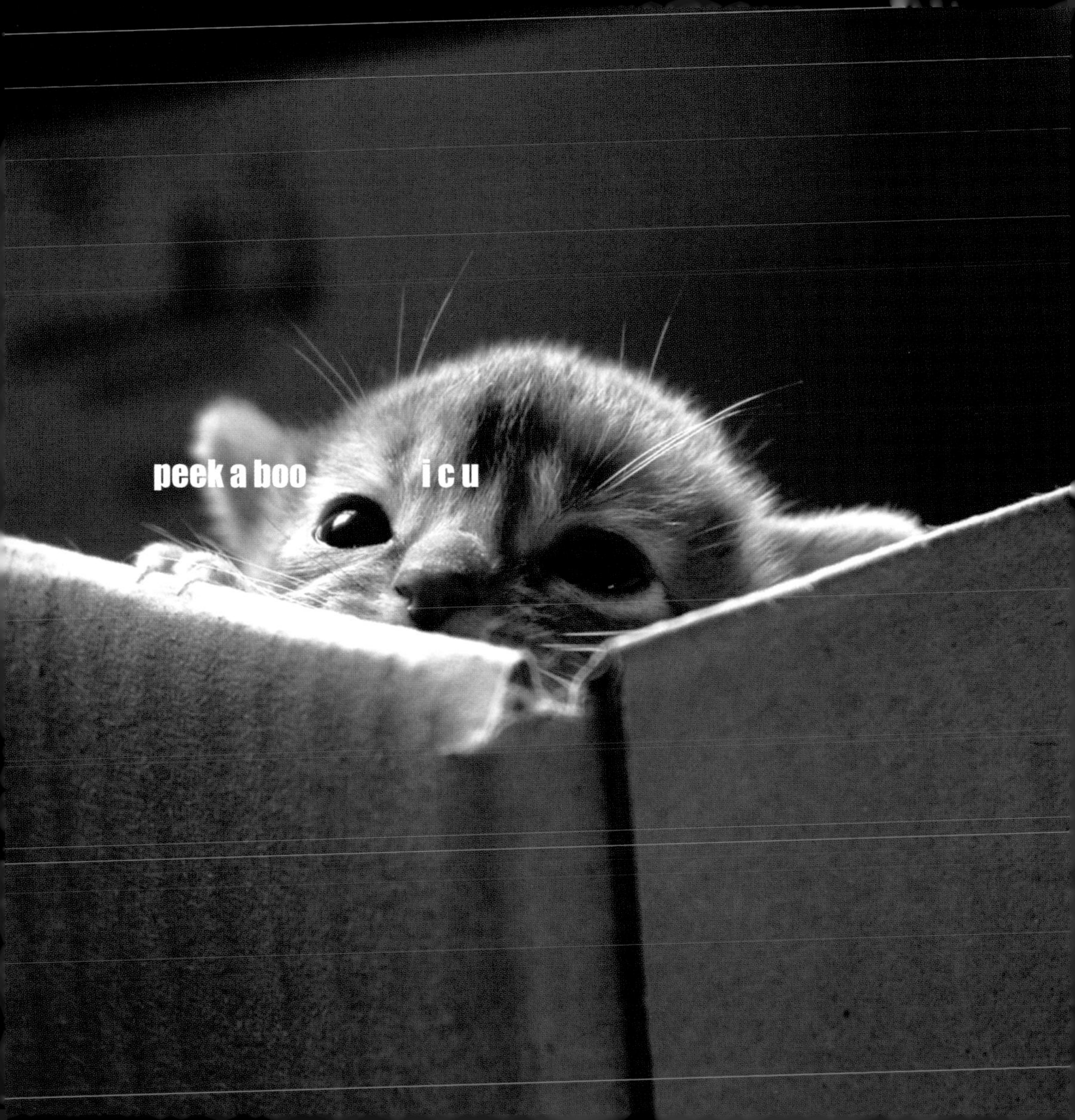
peek a boo
i c u

how can you say no to this face

olympic synchronized sleeping—
training in progress

Two servings of fruit, one serving of cute

No, ai can still feel da pea

invisible
cheezburger

den we warm ur heart.

KITTEH TO-DO LIST

Cause trouble

Yes   No

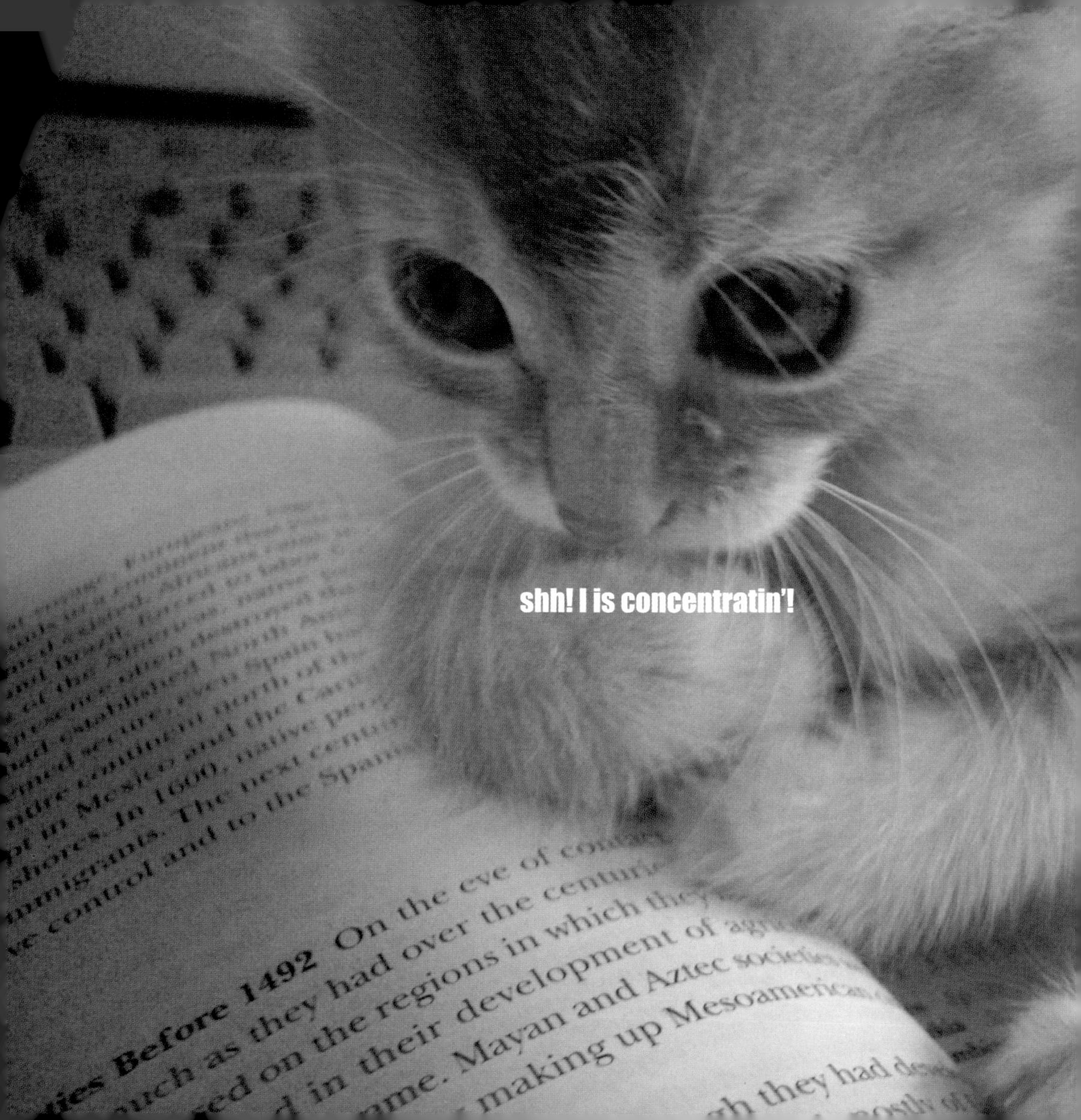
shh! I is concentratin'!

nap attack!!!

Day 96: no rescue in sight.
had 2 nom goober.

But I don't wanna haz a capshun

K, now read
forth line pleeze.

Yay i haz capshun

modist kitteh
covers hiz harblz

MOMCAT KNOWS BEST

Iz oks,
time outs no last forevers
Momma lets you out soon.

Dad kitteh put just a
drop of scotch on da kibble
now has quiet afternoon to nap

m, mom, mom, mom, mom, mom, mom, mom, m

UH-OH BAD KITTEH

lil basement cat
learns basic ebil

It was at this point that Alexander noticed the SECURITY CAMERA.

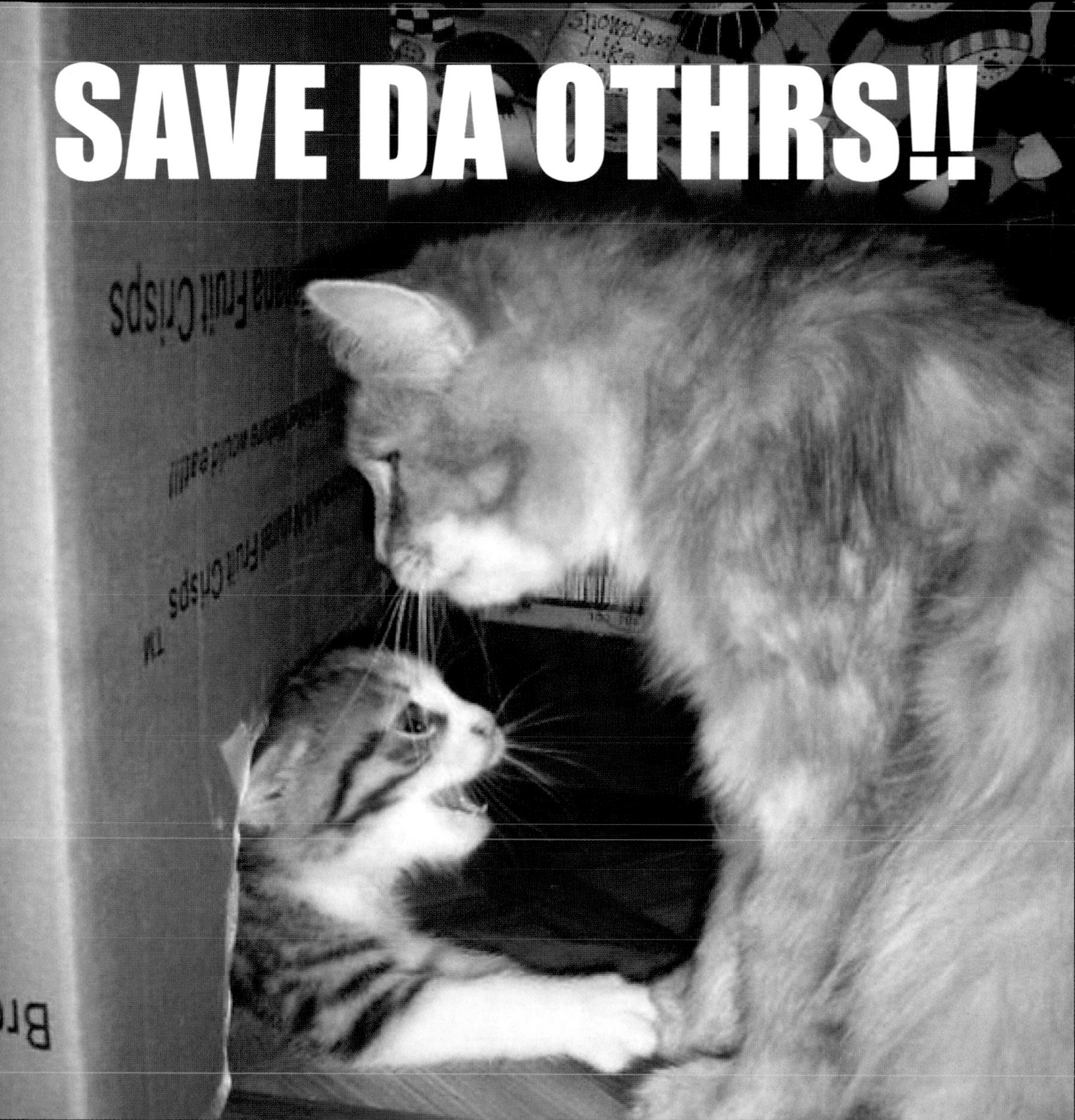
SAVE DA OTHRS!!

Iz done finking
is still googie's fault

No laugh . . . Iz really stuck

iz exawstin getin hoomin in carier

**Sun baff
better dan water baff any day.**

paranoid kitteh
cannot shake feeling of being watched

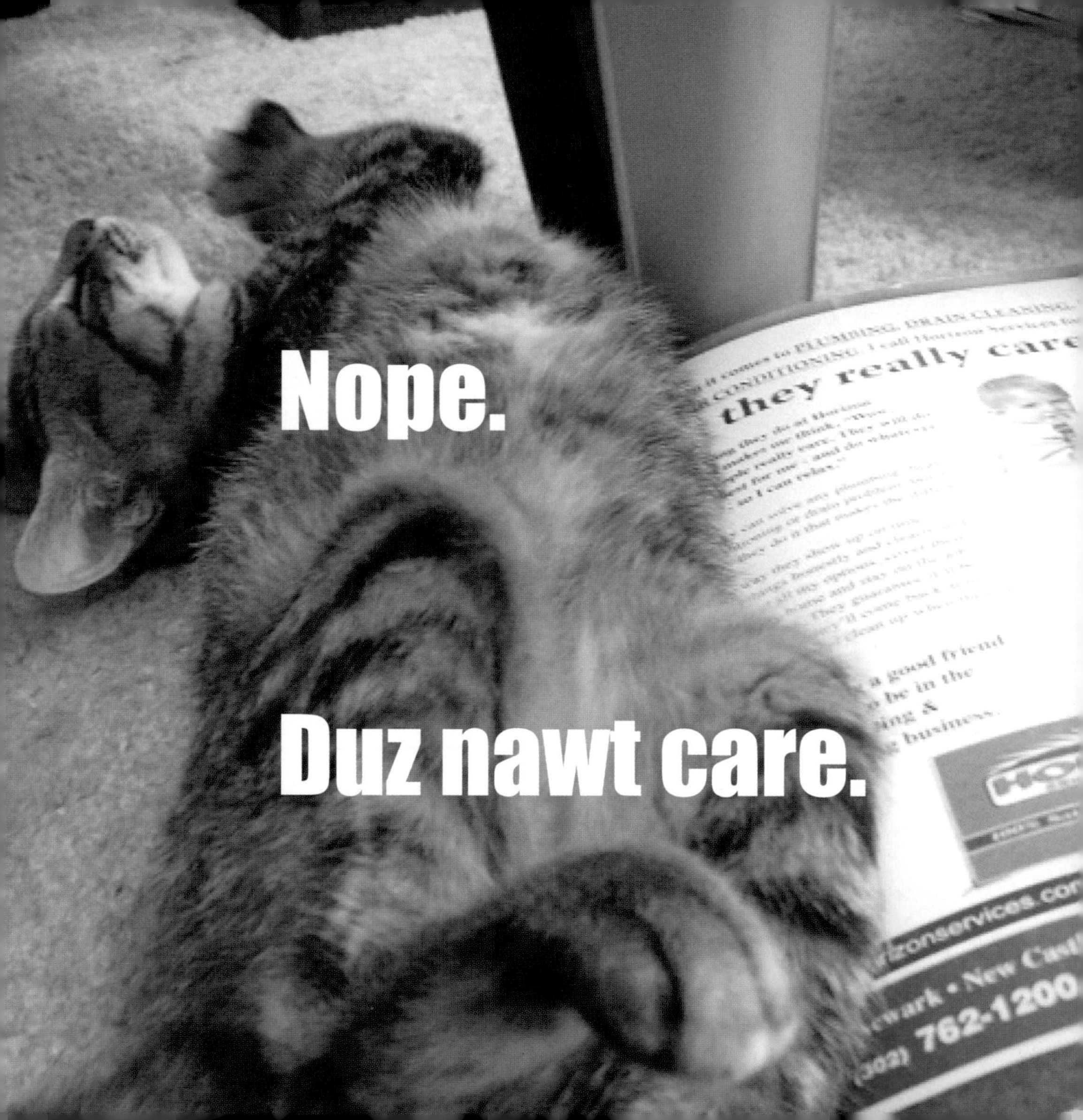
Nope.
Duz nawt care.

Paranoid Cats
Always sleep with one eye open

is not addicshun!
is just alwayz haz itz!

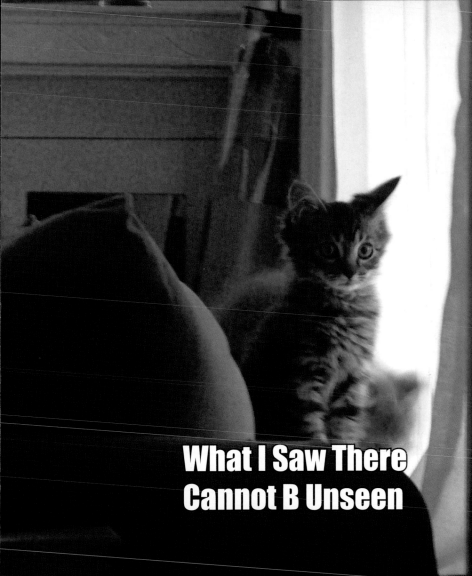

What I Saw There Cannot B Unseen

Hoominz comin'! Look feerce!

GIRLZ LUV A
BIKER KITTEH

Even Ceiling Cat can't protect against baths

ITTEH BITTEH KITTEH
COMMITTEH HALL OF FAME

FIELDTRIP!!!1!1
ai hafta uze teh litrbox
FREEDOM!!!
but, tahts MY sack lunch!
ow! ow! ow! ow!
?
Albert! Hurry up! wez missin ebryfing!
c'mon guyz! Ooooh, look! a frog!

ITTEH BITTEH KITTEH
CUDDL PUDDL COMMITTEH

Is our fort.
No gurlz allowd.

Itteh Bitteh Cheerleading
Committeh trying to wurk
on da piramids

Credits

PRODUCTION CREDITS:
Sonya Vatomsky and Ben Huh: Editing
Kittehs: Lookin' good!
Ben, Sonya, and the rest of Professor Happycat's staff would like to thank Patrick Mulligan, Travers Johnson, the Penguin team, our amazing agent Kate McKean and all of the kittehs and hoomins who made this book possible.

Thank you so much!

Image credits, by chapter:

Yr kitteh and u

LOLkitteh	Thx to
WARNING! Handheld device has been woken prematurely from sleep mode.	Mitzo by Riley Weber
I said I needz a drink . . . not a metal bowl wif water.	Schmerv wif speshul thx 2 hooman frenz Kristine an Josh an kat frenz Blanket an Omar
Antiques Roadshow Kitteh appraises your antiques	Gigi the Kitten by Beverly Art Studio www.thebeverlyartstudio.com www.gigithekitten.com
cute kitteh will kill you in ur sleepz	Oswald A.K.A. "Ozzy Monster" by Scott and Quel Lenker
crazy cat lady teh early years	Taylor and Nemo by Jamie D
I iz sizpicius of ur intenshuns	Larry Wong (hooman), Homer (kitteh)
Naow, go wayz . . . or I shall tawnt u a second tyme.	Miso by Michelle Pulsifer
Tutor Kitty is not pleased with your progress.	Fleur by Kira Schipper
OK, you can wash my blanky I guess but you have to promise to hold me while it's gone.	Michelle, Brian, Scotch, Merlin, and Mia
Halp . . . Iz ded . . . needz bellywubs 2 resurect	Gem by Nick, Laura, and Kristen
dis a joke, rite? U doan rly expect me to go crazy over a bunch o' ribbons 'n bells on a stick, right?	Gizmo by Gunner McGrath
U want to work?! U can't possibly want to work! I is sooo much more important and sooo much cuter!	Savannah, 12 weeks old, by Electrik Emily, Seattle, WA www.electrikemily.com
I noez what V-E-T spelz!	Chloe's kitteh by TessM
Bwaa ha ha ha . . . U haz date? No rly, what u do tonite?	Silas by Eichhorn
quit hoverin, I can't write wif u watchin me	Abby by Kate and her Dad
iz hanging upp bannur fer ur birfday	Photo by Peter Tirsek
He cantz get up heer, rite? I iz safe wif U, rite?	Shelby by Matt and Abby Thurman
My furs gradeskool yrbook foto	Kelly by Martha Colhoun
They suspect nothing.	Audrey Hepburn and MP (serving as pedestal), in conjunction with the girls who have been there since Day One: Momo, Neekee, and the Wingle. Love you all. Kthxbye.
U iz nice ur haws iz nice decide I own it all.	CCFCSPIT
we in ur tishus, aggrav8in ur alurgies.	Cooper and Bently by Delaina Olson

U no ur a kitteh person wen . . . . . . der r pillowz all ober ur haws in teh most peculiar places	Sevgul Sumer, Bas Dielemans, and Puck
Nao tellz me Hao duz dat make u feel?	Maggie, Josi, Fred, and Luci by Karol Harris
He cantz tawks nao But Iz happy to take mesage	Butch Catsidy and the Sundance Kat by Tami and Chris
no unnerstan— why u touch dis wen ai iz so soft?	Kris Hudson-Lee krishudsonlee.blogspot.com
Eye Exam: how many kitties do you see?	3 Members of Itteh Bitteh Kitteh Committee by Alixandria "Cat Mom" Andrews
BEATING GAS PRICES UR DOING IT WRONG	Sweetie Pie by Sabrina Bennett
Ders monsterz under mai bed kin I seep wif U?	Boo by Kelly and Manny
do ai haz to be happy?	Tambo by Zoe and Andy
Cat Starter Kit . . . . . Contents: 1	Matt, Charli, and Big Bailey
you got me for christmas	Pixie by Renee B and Jamie V
Your basket contains 6 items. Proceed to checkout?	Jeannette Greaves 4 Robert Burke wit KATitude :) www.flickr.com/photos/colormyworld/3589780322
No you not on the list I checked	Wolf by Jen Speed
Since u is already up, cud u gets me a drink of water? Fanks.	Algernon and Millie by Valerie Artigas

Kyootness: resistance is futile

LOLkitteh	Thx to
if cute doesn't work, we break out the nunchuks.	Mimie's Kittens
R U mai mudder? Seriously, that cat needs glasses.	Guiness by Todd and Erin
Make kyoot face, get treetz wurks evry tyme.	Tiger and Pinocchio by Sabrina Nussbaumer
shakespearean costume . . . on a budget	Scruffy by Wayne and Sarah Hershey
Iz only usin teh flip u can has teh flop	"Olive the Kitteh"—our little one—Erin Ogden and Jasper Boas (and Nabi too!)
Mak shur u uze da delicat cycle.	Iris by Sandra and Steven Beil
Dr. Tinycat's girlfrend Teeny	Maya by Emily and Paul Nelson
HAPPEE BIRFDAY! i guv yoo . . . ME!	Cocoa Puff, rescued by Cattitude, Inc www.njcattitude.org
First Kiss	Rocky and Luka by Jeff and Sanne
My Grandma . . . what a long nose you have.	Princess and kitten photo by Melissa Pearce / Attaway Borzoi

But how ai getz bak owt??	Peach by Alexander Quigley
True luv We gots it	Kista and Moon by Lowang and Zab00
I looks cute so you will feed me	Smudge by Chris Gin www.chrisgin.com
i has a pillow i has a blanket	Dan and Amy and Sophie Brady
Oh noes! Medusa gots him!	Purrfect Little Bear—Brenda (Mom); Davy (Dad); Beany (Iz tot youz eberythings youz nos but not eberythings Iz nos)
i has happee dreem	Fleur by Kira Schipper
Aagh! something just touched my paw!! no wait . . . it was just my other paw.	Maggie by Peggy Redle
ROAR!!!	Michelle, Brian, Scotch, Merlin, and Mia
He's behind me? Does he have a crazy look on his face?	Fatso and Whitefoot by Kathy Bays
PINK !? I HATE PINK!	Karissa and Callie Smith
I has a sad	Terry by RastaNisse
peek a boo i c u	Holly Ferguson
If I were any cuter I'd have to adopt myself	Mia by Elise Howarth, Australia
how can you say no to this face	No room for us. *sniff* In 72 hours we meet Ceiling Cat—by Romeow
I R DORABLEZ, YES I R!	Melody by Dida www.andreeam.net
as of now u r all . . . subjected . . . 2 meh cuteness	Misty Trawick
I has a paw.	Maggie, Josi, Fred, and Luci by Karol Harris
O hai, wurld!	Florida United Feline Friends, Inc.
olympic synchronized sleeping— training in progress	Duna and Elske by Sunny
Oh mai. I iz moar handsome den I thought.	Julia Gotz
Two servings of fruit, one serving of cute	Tigra by Sasha Amersek, Slovenia
No, ai can still feel da pea	Olivia Bear by Courtney Denning
Why yes, my name *is* Dusty.	Cece by Jenn Jacobs
invisible cheezburger	Luke by troymasonphotography.com
first we warm our butts den we warm ur heart.	Dawn Callari

Kitteh to-do list

LOLkitteh	Thx to
Cause trouble Yes No	Sweetpea by Willyboy Roy
I gots yoo nao yoo dastardly . . . yellow fing!	Ducktape attack by Hector
i haz no thumbz	Rachelle Last and Bossanova
Practical Joker Kitteh is turning off the hot water while you shower	Lucy by Patrick and Libby Pyo
Scotty . . . i can has beam?	Nellie Warms Her Butt by John Kessler
shh! I is concentratin'!	Ginger by Carolyn Chrisman
nap attack!!!	Zippo by Silke Greven
Day 96: no rescue in sight. had 2 nom goober.	Maggie's Kittehs by Jennifer Keith
vejetarian kitteh protectin hiz kill	Speck and corn by Jamie D
feet rubz pleeze?	Zorro by Janice, Lauren, and Jack Natovitch
Bow before your Master Good Dog	Yucca and Maverick (A.K.A. "Doofus") by Kimberly Huebbe
I see we meet again. . . .	Maverick by Katie and John McIlrath
Shhh . . . Iz watchin' mai storees . . .	Pompom by Janne Lindqvist
get 'em boyz	Oscar by Naomi Bousson

Teh artz of lol

LOLkitteh	Thx to
Be a LOLcat? I not shur	Hearthrug Black Faery, known as Mab, ruler of Jackie, Jon, and Daf.
But I don't wanna haz a capshun	Ragdoll kitten photo by Melissa Pearce / Attaway Borzol
Whoa! a capshun!	Chilli is the boss of Jodi and Paul Zaicos
K, now read forth line pleeze.	Blue and Sangria are kittens rescued by The Humane Society of Pensacola. Photograph by Karen Simenson.
Yay i haz capshun	Chi-Chiri by Jeffrey Ogershok
modist kitteh covers hiz harblz	Taters by Patrick and Misty Cavit

New and Improved! Now with LOLcat for extra humor!	Zoey Beans, Adriana, and Erik Mauer
plz someone press play	Pawse by Steven J. Morizio

Momcat knows best

LOLkitteh	Thx to
LOVE what life is all about	"Peaches" by Alayna Truttmann www.youtube.com/girlwithabook
Iz nice having teh kidz bak home for Thankzgivin Dinnur	Blaze and family by Paula Morhardt
No, Grasshoppur, u must wate until teh hoominz back iz turnd befoar u snatchz teh cheezburger.	Dawson and Emerson by Ginny Polek
OK, son, to catch the birdie.... Oooh, Shiney!	Teela and Guz, brought to you by Bonnie and Bindieye of Brisbane
You are NOT leaving the house dressed like that, young lady!	"Mellow" by Karen Griego
Ma! Tinky won't leave, an' I wuz heer first!	Cleopatra and Gizmo by Alissa Nagy
someday all dis will b urs	Felix and Wicket by Theresa Hudson Owner: Karen Mccarthy
Is oks, time outs no last forevers Momma lets you out soon.	Sami and Pili, the Malian kittehs, by Laura McPherson
Wat do u meen with "They ar yourz"?	Matt Conrad
Wh...wh...wot Is dis wunnerful stuf?! Ai skrachee an skrachee an skrachee.... If she lieks dat, she gonna luv da couch	In memory of Calypso, by Glen Eric Reed
Dad kitteh put just a drop of scotch on da kibble now has quiet afternoon to nap	Leona and her rescued kitties by Danella Lucioni
Typical, you pour yourself into making dinner there's always one who prefers a cheezburger	Destiny and kittens by Arlene Michelle
That's not a toy!	"Piper & Storm" by Rebecca DiLuzio
Hay Mom. Mom, mom, mom, mom, mom, mom, mom, mom, mom, mom.....mom, mom, mom, mom, mom, mom, mom, mom, mom, mom, mom, mom	CatmanSGA—Wolfyhound

Uh-oh bad kitteh

LOLkitteh	Thx to
No I iz not spy Y u ask?	Gandy: tiny and spoiled! by Elizabeth Thompson
lil basement cat learns basic ebil	Gandalf by Anna and David Scherer
Where did you hear a joke like that at your age??	Tiki y Nilo
Noo . . . wez not tawkin bout u . . .	ecaw n meemee by chaw
I'm ok.	Three unique kittens who have one mom, 2008. By Leo Arler.
Did u put file in cake?	Oliver the wonder kitteh by Sarah Hunt www.SarahHunt.com
I didn't do it And even if I did You wouldn't punish this face	Alden, by John, April, and Lillian Andrews
It was at this point that Alexander noticed the SECURITY CAMERA.	AbaGail by Roses Rags Cattery, Denver, CO
SAVE DA OTHRS!!	Baby Squee and Mama Fiona Squee by Sara Clevenger
Iz done finking is still googie's fault	Yamah by Saskia Suurling
Don't worry fren! Ima bust yoo out!	"Wolfie" by Judi Tafoya, Surgical Tech at Calista Animal Hospital in Las Cruces, NM
Why ai alwaez in troublez?? Ai triez to be good kitten . . .	Julie Falk
Srsly . . . no ask . . . jus halp plz . . . kthx	Kitty by Vince and Alisyah
No laugh. . . . Iz really stuck	Caligula by Frankenoid
Blah Blah Ceiling Cat . . . Something, something hand basket to Hell	Sharon Martin, author of "Sisters Forever," and son @ www.3amjosh.com
U shur dis saif? U bet. U not fall. Fall on feets if U do.	Libby Dog and Roscoe Cat by Steve and Morgan
A catapult? me no unnerstan	Bosco by Elurofila
you killed a man? I jus skrach sofa	Besito's Loveson of a Preacherman www.devons.se
iz exawstin getin hoomin in carier	Romeo by Jared Smith
Dis? It made frum teh pelts of our enemies	Maggie, Josi, Fred, and Luci by Karol Harris

Basement Cat can appear from anywhere. Even from your breakfast.	Yoda by Megan
mehehehehe . . . soon, very soon . . .	TewLucifer by Raven Z
everybodys stay calm! iz electrishun	Little Jack by Emily Busse and Giovannina Penze
Iz feel teh need . . . Teh need for speed!	Leon by Giuseppe Ciriolo
O krismas tree, O krismas tree ur bout to get destroyd	Dewey by Jessica Bucci
99% Evil 1% Milk	Circa "Il gatto molesto" by Frost
i killz it fer u no needz 2 thank me	Hailey by Amanda Nelson

Rules kittehs live bai

LOLkitteh	Thx to
Sun baff better dan water baff any day.	Gigi the Kitten by Beverly Art Studio www.thebeverlyartstudio.com www.gigithekitten.com
To katch teh cheezburger I muss *be* teh cheezburger.	Kogenta by Naoko
sigh EBERYFING I ebber owned or lubbed . . . is under teh fridge . . .	Gigi the Kitten by Beverly Art Studio www.thebeverlyartstudio.com www.gigithekitten.com
"Oil of old lady?" Smell like crazy cat lady to me!	Festus, proud owner of Margo and Jerry Davis
Iz theese lines moving? or has I had too much nip?	Polar Bear by Leah Breeding Kelly
Seems obvious to me that if I can read it then what it says ain't true!	Daisy Doodle by Matthew Barnes and Hannah Tammen
HALP! I can cleen myself you know!	Photo by Kelsie Groff
KITTEH RULE #1 Level of guilt directly proportional to cuteness displayed.	Wattson by Amanda Bober
New York kitteh Pays way 2 much for dis	Percival (Percy akshully) by pettur Laurie Foster
paranoid kitteh cannot shake feeling of being watched	CCFCSPIT

What do u mean, "Where's the present?" Can u not see this awesome BOX?	Otto by Trevor Turner
Nope. Duz nawt care.	Hannah aka Babycat the Genius Kitten and her owner (and photographer) Wendy (cartoonscats on the ICHC site!!)
Paranoid Cats Always sleep with one eye open	Ting Ting and Fan Tan by Shelly
is not addicshun! is just alwayz haz itz!	Marlo by Ashly
What I Saw There Cannot B Unseen	Dorian by Natalie and John Fritz
Hoominz comin'! Look feerce!	Arttu Vedenoja
GIRLZ LUV A BIKER KITTEH	To Sammy—"My not so little kitten/tiger"—Ryan Fitzgerald (Dad)
No assembly rekwired! Battrees not inkluded.	Ringo by Brittni at Brittni Linn Photography on Facebook
Even Ceiling Cat can't protect against baths	My little angel Runt (RIP) by Alana Jo

Itteh bitteh kitteh committeh hall of fame

LOLkitteh	Thx to
FIELDTRIP!!!1!1 but, tahts MY sack lunch! ow! ow! ow! ow! Albert! Hurry up! wez missin ebryfing! c'mon guyz! Ooooh, look! a frog! FREEDOM!!! ? ai hafta uze teh litrbox	Basket full of Kittehs by Krista Groff
Itteh bitteh kitteh committeh's bed is starting to get too itteh	Stardust's Kittehs by Sarah Hunt (www.SarahHunt.com)
ITTEH BITTEH KITTEH CUDDL PUDDL COMMITTEH	Photo by Diana MacLeod
Is our fort. No gurlz allowd.	Photo taken by Scott "SWAT" Strachan of our rescued kittehs. Dedicated to my mum for taking them in, and to my dad for putting up with my mum!
Stranger danger!1!!! STRANGER DANGER!!1!1!	Yalla and the kitties by Brieuc Mertens
itteh bitteh kitteh massage committeh	Bica Bogdan

it was YOU who turned the spin off?!	Joe, Diana, and Alex Richie of San Antonio
itteh bitteh kitteh mosh pitteh	"Kitty Pile" by Sara Kwasnicki
Itteh Bitteh Cheerleading Committeh trying to wurk on da piramids	Luana Bixby

WWW.SUMMERSDALE.COM